D1087739

CUTTING-EDGE STEM CAREERS™

Top STEM Careers in Math

CORONA BREZINA

ROSEN PUBLISHING®

New York

Published in 2015 by The Rosen Publishing Group, Inc.
29 East 21st Street, New York, NY 10010

Library of Congress Cataloging-in-Publication Data

Brezina, Corona.
Top STEM careers in math/Corona Brezina.—First
edition.
pages cm.—(Cutting-edge STEM careers)
Includes bibliographical references and index.
ISBN 978-1-4777-7676-6 (library bound)—ISBN 978-1-
4777-7678-0 (pbk.)—ISBN 978-1-4777-7679-7 (6-pack)
1. Mathematics—Vocational guidance—Juvenile
literature. I. Title.
QA10.5.B74 2015
510.23—dc23

2013038828

Manufactured in Malaysia

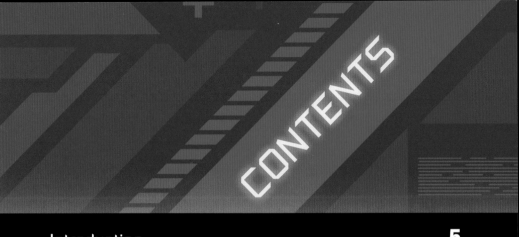

CONTENTS

S ay you're a recent college graduate with a degree in anthropology and archaeology, and you've already spent time at archaeological sites in Central America. What will you do with your future? Will you continue to investigate ancient civilizations in faraway locations, or will you instead turn to a career in... statistics?

Carrie Grimes chose statistics. She was fascinated by the potential of statistical analysis, in which raw data is examined in order to determine underlying patterns, relationships, and trends. Today, Dr. Grimes leads a research and technical team at Google, investigating what goes into making a truly effective search engine.

Statisticians solve practical problems by analyzing observational data and deriving relevant information that provides a solution. In an increasingly data-driven world, statisticians are in high demand.

Grimes isn't alone in her affinity for statistics. She chose a career path related to technology, but statistics is a broad field with applications in areas ranging from agriculture to zoology, with over two dozen other categories falling in between. They include biology, demography, economics, education, government, marketing, national defense, psychology, sports, telecommunications, transportation, and many others. The list was assembled by Statistics2013.org: International Year of Statistics. The event, supported by over 2,100 organizations in education, government, professional societies, and research organizations, aimed to promote a greater appreciation for how statistics benefits society.

Statistics is one of many in-demand fields that falls within the category of STEM careers—science, technology, engineering, and math. Many workers in STEM fields are highly skilled and educated. Grimes, for example, went on to earn a doctorate in statistics. Most STEM careers require a bachelor's degree, and prospects for advancement are enhanced by higher degrees. Fortunately, for young people interested in pursuing a STEM career, the government and various private groups are currently supporting various initiatives to increase participation in STEM areas.

The United States owes its current position as a global leader to the successes of its scientists and innovators of the twentieth century. But according to the U.S. Department of Education, only about 16 percent of American high school seniors are proficient in math and considering a STEM career. In general, American students have been falling behind their international peers in science and math scores.

Initiatives to increase the number of graduates in STEM fields provide exciting opportunities for young adults interested in pursuing a rewarding career with excellent job prospects for graduates. An economist recently told the financial magazine *Forbes*, "In the time of big data, many firms are looking for candidates who know their way around a statistical program and the scientific process." Given the stiff competition for the relatively few qualified workers, employers offer generous pay for candidates in STEM areas. Up-to-date information on salaries can be found in the Bureau of Labor Statistics (BLS) *Occupational Outlook Handbook*, available on line at the BLS Web site (http://www.bls.gov).

Graduates with degrees in mathematics or related majors are qualified for a variety of jobs across government, industry, finance, and education. In addition, many workers with a background in mathematics are employed in the other STEM categories of science, technology, and engineering. Mathematical expertise, as well as the analytical abilities and problem-solving skills honed by an education in math, can improve job prospects across a broad range of fields. Anyone pursuing opportunities in a STEM field related to mathematics will likely enjoy a rewarding and stimulating career. Those trained and employed in the STEM fields also have the satisfaction of knowing that their work plays a meaningful part in advancing American strength and influence within the global economy.

Math Class and Beyond

Mathematics is a common factor among all of the STEM career paths. Scientists study mathematical relationships in their research and use statistics to interpret and present their findings. Mathematical principles underpin every aspect of high-tech career fields, from computer science to telecommunication systems. Engineers of all types use advanced mathematics in designing devices and projects from artificial limbs to suspension bridges.

Much of the impact of mathematics on our daily lives occurs behind the scenes of our surroundings. You're probably sitting in a room of a building that was once nothing more than an architect's concept laid out in a set of blueprints, complete with dimensions and details of electrical and ventilation systems. Your town or city may have been shaped by an urban planner. It certainly owes its sense of order to a surveyor who plotted the land and set boundaries. If you make a banking transaction

Successful completion of a construction project requires mathematical proficiency throughout every stage, whether it's surveying the lot, designing the structure, or estimating the project's costs.

on your cell phone, you're utilizing the work of crypt-analysts who created the security features of the system. Meanwhile, far away in the physical build-ing of your financial institution, financial analysts are at work analyzing the best investments for the current economic climate. When you shop at the grocery store, your transactions at the cash reg-ister involve math, but so does the layout of the aisles and various departments, which may have been designed by an operations research analyst.

Applying Mathematics to One's Work

The field of mathematics is generally divided into applied and theoretical mathematics, although in practice the categories overlap. Most mathematicians work in careers involving applied mathematics. For them, mathematics is a valuable toolkit used to solve practical problems. One of the branches of mathematics with the broadest reach is statistics, which is applied in fields including science, social science, engineering, finance, health, and many others. Surveyors, architects, and urban planners utilize math to construct and modify the physical spaces in which we live. Physicists and astronomers use math to answer some of the most basic questions about the nature of our world and the infinite space beyond the earth.

Many careers in finance, insurance, accounting, and the financial operations of large corporations require solid math skills. Mathematics utilized in careers involving money go beyond adding and subtracting dollars and cents. People who work in

these areas may be required to interpret data, analyze statistics, or develop mathematical models, which

Many jobs in accounting and finance require close attention to detail, strong analytical skills, good organizational abilities, and technical facility with computers and various software programs.

require mathematical, problem-solving, and analytical abilities. These careers include accountants, auditors, and bookkeepers who maintain and prepare financial records for businesses large and small.

Cost estimators figure out the cost of manufacturing a product or completing a project. Financial analysts and financial managers make decisions on investments and corporate financial activities. Actuaries use advanced techniques in mathematics and probability to calculate the financial consequences of risk. Insurance underwriters decide whether to grant someone an insurance policy. Loan officers decide whether to grant someone a loan. Economists track how people and organizations use resources, goods, and services; analyze the implications; and make recommendations and forecasts.

A cryptanalyst uses math as a primary skill in breaking codes and creating new code systems to keep information secure. An operations research analyst solves problems related to the operations of large organizations. Math teachers share their enthusiasm for mathematics with students of all ages.

Finally, theoretical mathematicians conceive of new mathematical theories and relationships, with no consideration of practical applications. Nonetheless, applied mathematicians have put the work of theoretical mathematicians to good use. Forty years ago, certain areas of theoretical mathematics were dismissed as overly intellectual. Since then, they have proven to have practical value in disciplines such as physics, chemistry, astronomy, engineering, and biology.

Tackling Math

A recent publication by the Bureau of Labor Statistics discusses careers that use math and the competitive salaries earned by former mathematics majors. It points out, "Mastering mathematics is helpful in almost any career. Learning math helps workers analyze and solve problems—abilities that most employers value. And math teaches other important practices, including how to approach tasks methodically, pay attention to detail, and think abstractly." A solid mathematical background is an asset in a wide range of fields.

Nonetheless, people often think of math as difficult and frustrating. It's true that mastering mathematics can be challenging, but the reward of achievement and progress is worth the effort. Many of the negative associations about math actually stem from myths about the subject. For example:

Myth: Boys are better at math than girls.
Fact: Research has repeatedly disproved this claim.

Myth: Some people have a natural talent for math, and others lack aptitude for the subject.
Fact: Anybody with confidence, a positive attitude, and perseverance can master mathematics.

Myth: Math doesn't require intuition or creativity.
Fact: Everybody has a sense of intuition about math without realizing it, and the creative process is essential for making connections and gaining insights when doing research.

Myth: The point of math problems is to get the right answer.

Fact: Understanding the process for reaching the solution is the most important aspect of your math homework. Your teachers have a good reason for telling you to "show your work." In addition, there is sometimes more than one way to find the answer.

Myth: Math is mainly about repetition of drills and rote memorization of facts and formulas.

Fact: Approaching math with a problem-solving mindset is generally more effective than using a memorized procedure without understanding the concepts behind it.

Even if you find math difficult, remind yourself of why it's worth the effort. A huge number of career fields require some proficiency in math. Scientists, engineers, and computer scientists use math, of course, but so do doctors and nurses, lawyers and bankers, anthropologists and sociologists, artists and lawyers. In addition, statistics and numerical data are becoming more pervasive in our daily lives, and a basic understanding of mathematical concepts is necessary to stay in touch with the trends and social issues that have a daily influence upon us.

STEM and Education

STEM career opportunities are projected to increase significantly in the United States through 2020, yet

As policy makers and educators have grown concerned about the lack of STEM student preparedness, they have introduced innovative programs and explored new teaching methods to spur interest in STEM fields.

not enough young Americans are pursuing expertise in these areas. According to a recent report by My College Options/STEMconnector, high school seniors were 10 percent less likely to express interest in a STEM career than were high school freshmen.

To policy leaders, this trend represents a failure in the educational system. In order to boost interest and aptitude in science, the federal government has encouraged a range of STEM initiatives. A key element is recruiting and training 100,000 teachers in STEM subjects. The STEM strategy also calls for more hands-on activities that engage and hold students' interest in STEM areas. Another key aspect is targeting groups that are underrepresented in STEM occupations, such as women, minorities, and first generation Americans.

These initiatives mean that students have abundant educational options and support in STEM areas as they complete their high school education. A solid background for a career in mathematics begins with taking as many math and computer science classes as you can. Talk with your teachers about how you can further explore your interest in math during your free time. Take English classes as well, since good written and verbal communication skills are essential in many fields related to mathematics. Don't limit your interests during high school—many subjects involve a mathematical component that might not be immediately apparent. All of the natural sciences are closely linked with mathematics. Psychology and social sciences are relevant to mathematics-related careers as various as actuary, cryptanalyst, statistician, and urban planning. Business and economics classes provide a good

THE IDEAL INTERNSHIP

An internship is a great way to acquire on-the-job experience that will stand out when you list it on your résumé. Internships are temporary trainee positions for high-school students, college and graduate students, and recent graduates. They can last for a summer, a semester, a year, or maybe just for a month between college semesters. An internship benefits both the intern, who gains valuable practical knowledge and skills, and the employer, who gets the labor and enthusiasm of the intern. An intern may also make useful professional connections during the internship. Companies sometimes hire interns permanently after their period of internship ends—the employers know that the former intern is competent and already experienced in the job.

A hunt for an internship is very similar to a job search. It requires research, networking, and sending out applications tailored to the needs of each employer. Unlike an entry level job, however, an internship may be either (lowly) paid or unpaid. Even in the U.S. Senate, only about a third of senators pay their interns. For a low-income student, the prospect of taking on financial responsibility for housing and living expenses during an unpaid internship can be daunting.

In addition, some employers have been accused of exploiting their interns, requiring them to work long hours with low or no pay and without providing useful training in the field. Most internships are legitimate and provide substantial career benefits, but research your prospective employer and familiarize yourself with the U.S. Department of Labor's standards for unpaid internships.

background for many of the careers involved in finance and accounting.

Look for extracurricular activities related to STEM subjects, such as math club, science Olympics, and science fairs. The recent STEM initiatives have increased opportunities for middle school and high school students—the Girl Scouts have even introduced a STEM program. But you shouldn't limit yourself to math and technology-related pursuits. Try taking up interests such as volunteer work, the debate team, or drama club, which will give you a well-rounded high school experience.

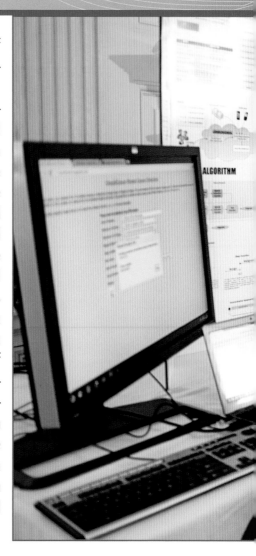

Planning for College

Almost all STEM careers in math require a bachelor's degree. A master's degree will improve one's chances of advancement. The national level STEM initiatives aim to increase STEM graduates by one million by the year

President Barack Obama congratulates Brittany Wenger, a participant in the 2013 White House Science Fair, which showcased the winners from a broad range of STEM competitions from across the United States.

2020. They include measures—such as scholarships, fellowships, and support programs—to encourage undergraduates in STEM majors and graduate students pursuing higher degrees in STEM fields.

For example, some measures encourage first and second year students to continue their STEM studies when they're tempted to switch majors. Scholarships and other resources are available from government organizations such as the National Science Foundation, as well as from private companies, foundations, and nonprofit organizations. Some scholarships are targeted toward certain demographics, such as women or minorities, and some apply to students pursuing a specific major. STEM initiatives are constantly expanding and evolving, so continue researching scholarship and grant prospects throughout the course of your education.

As you're pursuing your interest in mathematics, you should keep your long-term career goals in mind. A degree in mathematics or statistics will provide you with a solid background for a wide variety of jobs related to math. Your college and academic department will be able to provide you with career pointers as you near graduation and begin thinking about your first job out of school. But some career areas related to math benefit from a specialized major. If your dream is to become an actuary or an architect, for example, you should probably choose a school that offers a major in actuarial science or architecture. Research your career fields of interest thoroughly when you're choosing a college and academic program.

You also might earn a bachelor's degree with a broad major such as mathematics, statistics, computer science, business, or economics, and then pursue a graduate degree in a narrower field. Many urban planners and operations research analysts, for example, earn a bachelor's degree and then pursue a master's degree in the field. In some career areas, especially those in research and academia, a master's degree or a doctorate is required for even entry level positions. Many professionals return to school from the workplace in order to earn higher degrees, which increases their expertise and enhances future career prospects.

Putting Math to Wo
Careers in Industrial and
Applied Mathematics

areers in industrial and applied mathematics use the mathematical toolkit to solve practical problems in the real world. A huge number of occupations require that workers measure, calculate, quantify, compute, or model data in the course of their daily activities. In fact, mathematics is a unifying factor in all STEM jobs—practically every career in science, technology, and engineering also requires solid math skills.

Mathematics is essential in a diverse range of disciplines. It might seem that the careers of architect and astronomer have little in common, just as urban planners and physicists may seem worlds apart from each other. But all of the careers in this section are grounded in mathematical principles and processes. They all require mathematical proficiency as well as the critical thinking and problem-solving skills that are developed by mastering mathematics. Math skills provide people with the tools to understand and interpret the numbers, patterns, and data that are central to many modern career fields.

Statistician

Statistics is the science of learning and solving problems using observational data. Statisticians are employed in every field that involves numerical data, and that includes a huge variety of possible career paths. Statisticians make predictions about economic growth,

Statisticians use mathematical and statistical methods to produce accurate, unbiased data that can be used to determine whether a prediction is trustworthy or whether information is correct.

NATE SILVER: SUPERSTAR STATISTICIAN

In 2008, the young statistician Nate Silver wasn't impressed by media analysis of the upcoming presidential election. Polls and demographic data had the potential to forecast the likely outcomes for political races, but nobody was crunching the numbers appropriately, accurately, or thoroughly enough. Silver seized the moment, launching a blog called FiveThirtyEight. He took the name from the number of electoral votes cast in a presidential election.

Silver developed a statistical model that analyzed polling data and other factors that influence election results. He constantly updated his projections as election day neared. His formula proved stunningly accurate. In 2008, Silver correctly predicted the vote of 49 out of 50 states. He was only off by 1 percent in his prediction of the popular vote.

FiveThirtyEight became even more popular and influential. Silver's projections were closely watched during the 2012 election. At this time, the blog was affiliated with the *New York Times*. Once again, Silver's forecasts triumphed. In 2012, Silver wrote a book called *The Signal and the Noise: Why So Many Predictions Fail—but Some Don't*. In 2013, he announced that FiveThirtyEight was moving from the *New York Times* to ESPN.

Silver showed an interest in math and statistics from an early age, and he earned a degree in economics from the University of Chicago in 2000. He honed his expertise in statistics developing the Player Empirical Comparison and Optimization Test Algorithm (PECOTA), which revolutionized forecasts for the performance of teams and players.

Nate Silver gives a presentation at the 2013 SXSW Interactive Festival in Austin, Texas. Silver applies statistical analysis to politics, sports, and even airline arrival and departure times.

consult with corporations about consumer interest in new products, study public health trends, and interpret the data for scientific research papers. By examining the data, they reveal patterns that offer explanations about why something happened and what is likely to happen in the future.

A statistical analysis begins with the collection of data, which may include the development of surveys and a determination of a valid sample size. Some statisticians collect their own data, but many are provided with raw data to interpret. The Census Bureau, for example, employs thousands of workers who gather demographic information for the government. Statisticians analyze the data, providing results that are crucial for determining representation in the government, the allocation of funds to communities, and much more.

Much of a statistician's time is spent on a computer performing data analysis. Computer software utilizes statistical models that organize, manipulate, and interpret data. The statistician may present his or her findings in the form of tables, charts, graphs, or written reports.

Good communication skills are crucial for statisticians. Many statisticians work as part of a team. They may also cooperate with workers who collect data and experts in fields unfamiliar to the statistician. This may require a crash course in subjects from nuclear safety and crop management to crime prevention. In addition, statisticians must be able to present their conclusions in language that is accessible to nonstatisticians.

There are two general types of statisticians: mathematical statisticians and applied statisticians. Mathematical statisticians study the theory behind statistics and develop new statistical models. Applied statisticians—who make up most of the field—use mathematical tools to make sense of nuts-and-bolts questions and problems.

Statisticians work in areas ranging from chemistry and engineering to psychology and sports, but the largest numbers of statisticians are employed by the government (including the military), the health care industry, and manufacturing. Almost all government agencies employ statisticians who track demographic, economic, scientific, environmental, and agricultural trends. Statisticians in health-related fields analyze statistics pertaining to public health, medicine, and pharmaceuticals. Statisticians working in industry are involved with every stage of manufacturing a product, from development and testing to marketing and pricing.

A statistician may have a specialized job title indicating a focus in a particular field. Econometricians, for example, study economic data. Biostatisticians or biometricians study health data.

Most statisticians major in mathematics or statistics in college, but a degree in computer science or economics can also provide a good background for a career as a statistician. A double major or a minor in subjects such as engineering, biology, business, or health sciences can be useful for work in specialized fields. A bachelor's degree is required for most entry-level positions, and higher-level positions may require a master's degree or Ph.D.

Training in statistics provides a good background for a number of related careers. Market research analysts, for example, study market conditions for products and services and help companies understand what consumers will buy and why they will do so (and, likewise, what they won't buy and why). Survey researchers design and conduct surveys and analyze survey data.

Surveyor

Surveyors establish and verify official land, airspace, and water boundaries. They collect exact measurements of data such as the location, shape, contour, height, and dimensions of land or land features. Surveying is a time-honored profession—surveyors sometimes remind people that three of the four figures featured on Mount Rushmore were surveyors.

Many surveyors spend a great deal of time in the field. They use hi-tech tools such as GPS as well as more traditional instruments, such as the theodolite, transit, levels, and distance measuring devices. Geographical information is also collected from planes and satellites. Surveyors are often required to verify previous surveys by researching land deeds and locating old boundary

A surveyor at a building site looks through the telescope of a theodolite, an instrument that measures angles. Many modern versions of this centuries-old instrument incorporate electronic and computerized components.

lines and markers. Surveying also involves time spent indoors on a computer, since surveyors prepare maps and reports based on the data they collect.

Surveying measurements are used in many fields related to the use of land, airspace, and water. Surveyors establish property lines and define airspace for airports. They are among the first workers on a construction or engineering site. They describe the boundaries for mining and logging projects. They map areas affected by disasters such as oil spills in order to help the cleanup effort. Surveyors' data is used in drawing up legal documents such as deeds and leases, and surveyors are sometimes called on as expert witnesses in court.

Many surveyors specialize in a specific area, such as land or boundary surveying, highway surveying, and surveying for mining or petroleum exploration, which requires exploration below the earth's surface. Topographical surveyors prepare topographical maps that show the surface features of a site. Geodetic surveyors map large areas of the earth's surface using GPS data. Marine or hydrographical surveyors measure the area, depth, and shape of the land under bodies of water. Photogrammetrists take aerial photos of large areas and create 3-D maps of the features of the land.

Good communication skills are essential for surveyors. A surveyor taking measurements in the field often supervises a surveying crew. Surveyors also work closely with architects and engineers in drawing up plans for a site. They may consult with urban and regional planners, cartographers, oceanographers, and government officials.

Math skills are crucial for a surveyor, especially in algebra, geometry, and trigonometry. Surveyors must also possess the ability to visualize the spatial rela-

A surveyor holds a surveying pole on a beach in Fort Pierce, Florida, during a shore protection project, in order to measure erosion. Some surveyors specialize in environmental surveying.

tionships of geographical features in their minds. A surveyor must pay close attention to detail and have good problem-solving skills. Unlike many jobs related to mathematics, surveying requires physical fitness, coordination, and keen eyesight. Surveyors may be required to travel for the job.

A job as a surveyor generally requires a bachelor's degree in a major such as surveying technology or engineering. Some technical colleges offer associate's degrees in surveying. In addition, most states require surveyors to be licensed, generally by the National Council of Examiners for Engineering and Surveying. Applicants must pass exams and gain work experience under the supervision of a licensed surveyor. Some professional associations also offer certification in specialized areas of surveying.

Surveyors are assisted by surveying technicians who operate the instruments in the field. Many surveying technicians learn their duties on the job, although some complete vocational training or earn an associate's degree. Professional certification is also offered for surveying technicians.

Architect

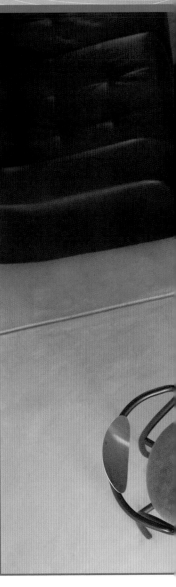

Architects plan, design, and oversee the construction of buildings and other structures. Their work is behind the concept, layout, and appearance of homes and retail stores, arenas and office buildings, industrial parks and apartment complexes, and train stations and hospitals. Some architects work on landscaping or the layout of new housing subdivisions.

Architects may have models constructed in order to study the three-dimensional relationships among different components of a project. Models may also be displayed to clients and the public.

You might imagine that an architect spends most of his or her workday perfecting designs of projects, but architects actually spend a great deal of time dealing with the business aspect of the job. Excellent com-

Prestigious architects and architectural firms are internationally in demand. These futuristic eco-friendly "farmscrapers" were designed by a French firm for the Chinese city of Shenzhen.

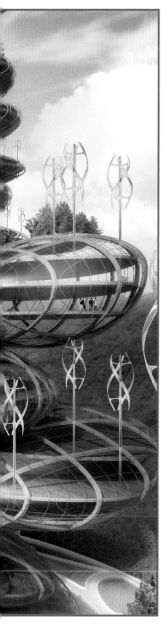

munication skills are essential for an architect. Architects have to "sell" their work to prospective clients and convince them that their vision can be a successful one. Once a client has hired an architect, he or she prepares preliminary plans based on the client's needs. A design must both satisfy the client's requirements and meet safety and zoning codes. The final design is presented in the form of blueprints prepared on a computer that show a detailed layout as well as structural and engineering specifics. The architect also prepares drawings that project what the completed building will look like. Sometimes he or she also builds a model.

Before construction begins, the architect may consult with surveyors, environmental impact specialists, engineers, and other experts about the site and plans. The architect sometimes helps the client hire builders and negotiate the contract. Once the project is under construction, the architect works with the contractors to ensure that the work is proceeding according to the plans. Often, unexpected factors, such as new building and safety codes or cost overruns, may require revision of some aspects of the plans.

Many architects specialize in a specific type of work. They may focus on renovating interiors or working on large civil-engineering projects. Environmentally friendly "green" designs are increasingly in demand.

Architects generally earn a bachelor of architecture degree, which usually takes five years to complete. Some architects go on to earn a master's degree. After graduating, new architects spend three years under the supervision of experienced architects, usually as part of an internship. During this period, they perform duties such as drafting, researching zoning laws and other legal matters, and revising existing plans. After completing the internship, they are eligible to take the Architect Registration Exam, which is required for obtaining a license. Some architects also choose to pursue certification by the National Council of Architectural Registration Boards (NCARB).

Architects are assisted by drafters and computer-aided design (CAD) technicians who use software to convert the designs of engineers and architects into technical drawings and plans.

Urban Planner

Urban planning, also called city planning, involves the crafting and designing of plans, projects, and programs for land use. Urban planners decide what types of buildings are appropriate for a neighborhood and develop transportation networks. They suggest ways to

Urban and regional planners make recommendations that will serve the short-term and long-term public good. They may need to balance the conservation of natural resources with plans for new development.

make public spaces more accommodating and to encourage commercial activity in business districts. The ultimate goal of urban planning is to create a healthy, safe, and prosperous community that promotes a high quality of life among its citizens. Often, urban planners are consulted when leaders are trying to revitalize an area or steer future growth.

Urban planners often specialize in a specific subfield. Some focus on land use and enforcing zoning policies. Transportation planners analyze the demand for services and predict future transportation needs. Environmental and natural resource planners focus on preserving and improving natural resources and encouraging sustainable functioning of an area.

An urban planner must possess a broad and varied skill set. Mathematical and analytical skills are very important in the job. Urban planners analyze the demographic statistics of an area when working on a project. This includes data such as the population breakdown and needs for various services. An urban planner must have the ability to visualize the spatial dimensions and relationships of an area, always keeping in mind details such as building density and transportation corridors. Urban planners may create maps and models on the computer and draft financing and budget proposals.

Urban planners are charged with developing plans that will take into account a community's needs years and even decades into the future. But they must also convince leaders, developers, economic consultants, special interest groups, and the public that their plan will lead to an improved quality of life. Discussion of urban development projects can be contentious and highly emotional. Good communication skills are crucial for an urban planner. They need to be able to address citizens' concerns and persuade people to recognize the benefits of their proposed plan. An urban planner may be called on to act as a mediator between opposing points of view on an issue.

Most urban planners hold a master's degree. A bachelor's degree in economics, geography, political science, or environmental design provides good preparation for a job in urban planning. Urban planners can pursue certification in the field from the American Institute of Certified Planners. Over half of all urban planners are employed by local governments. Others work for state governments or for private employers such as real estate developers. A related career is that of regional planner. Regional planners consider plans, projects, and programs for large areas of land—far more territory than a single urban neighborhood—potentially encompassing urban, suburban, and rural areas.

Physicist

Physicists study all aspects of matter and energy in the natural world. They try to determine the mechanisms that make the universe work, from the properties of the smallest particles of matter to the movements of far-away galaxies. Physicists use their expertise to develop new theories and technologies. Their breakthroughs have led to the development of many products we now take for granted, from microwave ovens to the lasers used in surgery.

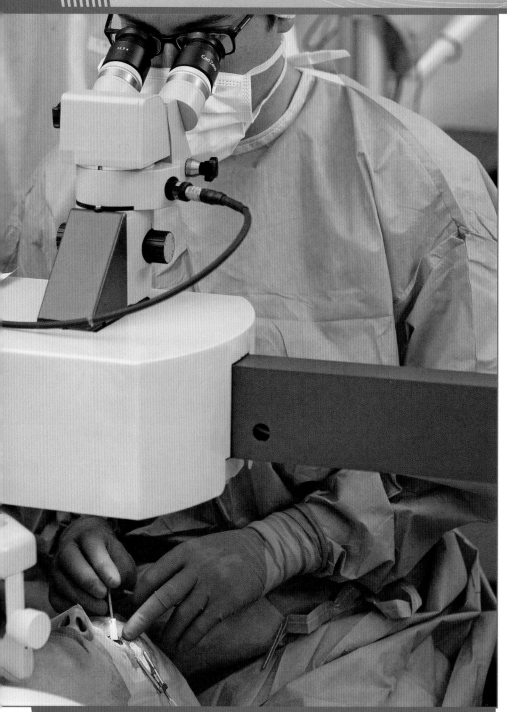

A surgeon performs eye surgery using an excimer laser, a powerful and precise tool that uses pulses of light to cut through tissue. Physicists tested the first lasers during the 1960s.

Most physicists focus on theoretical physics, experimental physics, or applied physics. Theoretical physicists produce theories that explain the workings of the natural world, often using such complex mathematics that their models are impossible to test experimentally. Theoretical physicists generally concentrate in a highly specialized subfield of physics.

Experimental physicists design and implement experiments that test theories and reveal previously unknown properties of matter and energy. Much of their work is done in laboratories and research facilities using highly specialized equipment. Some of the most exciting twenty-first century breakthroughs in physics have been produced by the Large Hadron Collider, started up in 2008, at the European Organization for Nuclear Research (CERN). Researchers at CERN study interactions between the fundamental particles that make up matter by causing them to collide at nearly the speed of light.

Applied physicists use their knowledge of physics to develop and improve products and applications ranging from circuit boards to improved weather models. Many applied physicists work on developing advanced equipment, such as medical devices and telecommunications technology.

The laws of physics are relevant to every branch of science and technology, and physics is a highly interdisciplinary pursuit. Some physicists specialize in subfields that overlap with another discipline. Biophysicists apply the laws of physics to living things; geophysicists study the physics of the earth. In addition, expertise in physics can be relevant to many nonscientific fields.

In 2008, the first beam, finer than a human hair, was steered around the 18 mile (27 km) circumference tunnel that makes up the world's most powerful particle accelerator at CERN.

According to the American Physical Society, knowledge in physics is beneficial in engineering, medicine, law, business, finance, education, writing, and a variety of technical careers.

Most jobs involving theoretical or experimental physics require a Ph.D. Many research physicists also teach at universities. Applied physics positions require at least a master's degree. Many applied physicists work in industry or research and development facilities. The government—especially the Departments of Defense, Energy, and Commerce—employs a significant number of physicists. Candidates with a bachelor's degree are qualified for jobs as research assistants or for careers that draw upon a knowledge of physics.

Students interested in pursuing physics should take advantage of all of the math and science courses and extracurricular activities available in high school. A college physics major requires many advanced math courses, as well as courses in physics and computer science. Physicists should be prepared to work as part of a research team along with other scientists, engineers, technicians, and students.

Astronomer

Astronomers study objects found in outer space throughout the universe. Some astronomers focus on the objects within the solar system, such as the sun, planets, asteroids, and comets, and examine their properties and movements. Other astronomers investigate galaxies, quasars, black holes, and other celestial objects that exist many light years distant from the earth. Some astronomers try to answer fundamental questions about the nature of matter and energy and how the universe came to exist. Astronomy is a huge field, and most astronomers focus on a specific area of study. Astrophysicists specialize in using the principles of physics to examine topics in astronomy. Today, the terms "astrophysicist" and "astronomer" are nearly interchangeable, since most astronomers use physics in their work.

Astronomy is unique among the sciences in that it relies almost totally on observation rather than experimentation. Similar to the field of physics, however, astronomy is divided into theoretical astronomers who propose models and observational astronomers who seek to answer questions or test theories. In past centuries, astronomers might be found staying up all night peering through a telescope. Today, the giant optical telescopes, radio telescopes, satellites, and spacecraft that collect data are operated by computers. Some astronomers still spend their nights in observatories, but most of their time is spent at the computer analyzing data.

The largest number of astronomers hold teaching and research positions at universities and colleges. They are often affiliated with observatories and research laboratories as well. The government employs about a third of all astronomers—many work for the National Aeronautics and Space Administration (NASA) and other agencies. A small proportion of astronomers work in business or private industry.

The field of astronomy is small and highly competitive. A Ph.D. is absolutely required in order to find a job, and many astronomers spend years doing postdoctoral work before landing a permanent position.

Despite the competition and required years of education, astronomy continues to exert a fascination for many people. But the "Ask an Astronomer" team at Cornell University encourages astronomy lovers to follow their dream: "If astronomy is what you really want to do, go for it! If you are willing to be flexible, it is unlikely that you will end up unemployed."

Prospective astronomers must have a high aptitude in math, science, and computers. Since astronomy is a competitive field, good grades are also necessary to be accepted for top programs and projects. Research is important for advancement at every level. The "Ask an Astronomer" team suggests that high-school students thinking about college "look for one that offers an astronomy major (not just a minor) and ask about undergraduate opportunities for research." In addition, astronomers should have strong written and verbal communication skills. Regardless of specialization, most astronomers write papers and give lectures throughout the course of their career.

CHAPTER THREE

Money Matters

Careers in Finance, Accounting, and Insurance

The world of business offers a multitude of career opportunities for anyone with mathematical aptitude. Finance professionals work for banking institutions, insurance companies, government agencies, and accounting departments of businesses large and small. Career options involving money include positions for a variety of mathematical skill levels. Actuaries, for example, must take extensive advanced math classes in college, while bookkeepers must be able to perform basic math functions with a high degree of accuracy. Regardless of the specific position, a background in mathematics tends to promote a logical, problem-solving mind-set. This will be an asset in a career spent analyzing budgets, tracking financial operations, or sifting through statistical data related to investments.

If you're an aspiring accountant, analyst, or other business professional, you may choose to pursue a college degree in finance, business, or a relevant specialized major such as actuarial science. Or you can complete a mathematics degree while taking business courses as well. Internships provide excellent opportunities for gaining perspective on different areas of business and finance as you choose a particular field of interest. In addition, prospective employers are likely to look favorably on candidates with experience in the field.

Accountant and Auditor

Accountants and auditors keep track of financial records. Accountants oversee financial operations, monitor profits and losses, and compute taxes and ensure that they are paid on time. They also prepare reports on an organization's financial health, which managers consult when making business decisions. An accountant may develop a new accounting or bookkeeping system or modify an existing one. Auditors are specialized accountants who examine and verify the accuracy of financial records.

Most accountants fall within four main categories. Public accountants provide accounting, tax, auditing, and consulting services for individuals and organizations. Management accountants work for organizations such as large companies. They prepare financial records for internal use. Government accountants keep financial records for federal, state, and local governments. They also audit the records of private businesses and individuals. Internal auditors verify the financial records of a company, checking for accuracy,

In recent years, accountants' duties have expanded to include a greater range of responsibilities as technological advances have eliminated much of the rote work associated with the field.

waste, fraud, and mismanagement. There are many specialties within these four categories—an accountant may focus on a particular area such as budget accounting, tax accounting, or property accounting.

Accountants and auditors work standard forty-hour weeks in an office, although some overtime may be required in the beginning of the year during tax season. The largest proportion of accountants work for accounting, tax preparation, bookkeeping, and payroll service firms. But accounting services are required by individuals and organizations of all types, from small businesses and huge corporations to charities and labor unions.

Solid math skills, an attention to detail, and good organizational skills are absolutely necessary in the field. Accounting work is sometimes viewed as monotonous and routine, but the job sometimes requires problem-solving and detective work to analyze the data. Good communication skills are also necessary. Accountants often work as part of a team, and they must be prepared to present clear facts and figures to their clients.

A career as an accountant or auditor generally requires a bachelor's degree with a major in accounting. Many accountants also complete additional coursework and take the challenging four-part CPA exam to become a certified public accountant. Sometimes accountants fulfill the requirement for additional coursework by earning a master's degree. Additional types of certification are also available, such as CMA (certified management accountant) and CIA (certified internal auditor). Specific requirements for certification vary from state to state.

Many accountants begin their careers by completing summer internships in an accounting firm during college. If their work is satisfactory, they may be offered a position as an associate in the company upon graduating. Accounting is a high-demand field, and accountants can combine their expertise with other interests. On its career site, the American Institute of Certified Public Accountants describes career options for accountants related to entertainment, technology, sports, education, criminal investigation, the environment, travel, and food and fashion.

Bookkeeper

Bookkeepers, also called bookkeeping clerks, handle the financial records of a business or other organization. Bookkeepers produce finan-

cial statements and reports. They enter, compute, and verify numerical information about transactions. They may handle payments to banks, track inventory, and manage payroll of employees. Their work indicates the bottom line of how a company is faring financially.

Most bookkeepers manage financial records and statistics for smaller firms rather than large companies. They record daily business transactions and prepare statements reflecting the firm's performance.

Bookkeeping is not the same as accounting. Although bookkeepers and accountants both deal with financial records, accounting encompasses a much broader range of responsibilities than bookkeeping. Accountants analyze financial data, compile reports such as tax returns based on a bookkeeper's data, verify the accuracy of records, and design bookkeeping systems. Bookkeepers manage the day-to-day financial records and prepare financial statements and returns for use within the company.

Bookkeepers often work for smaller businesses and institutions rather than large corporations. A bookkeeper for a small firm may be solely responsible for every aspect of maintaining a financial record-keeping system.

A bookkeeper must be detail-oriented, methodical, and highly organized. Since most bookkeeping systems are computerized, proficiency with computers is necessary, especially in programs using spreadsheets and databases. Although the level of math required for the job is not particularly high, accuracy and solid basic skills are essential. Good communication skills are also required for the job. A bookkeeper must be able to translate technical financial jargon into plain terms. In addition, a bookkeeper must maintain records of the financial activities of all the employees in the business. Effective communication helps the bookkeeper keep track of the necessary financial documents.

Bookkeepers must have a high school diploma, and employers look for candidates who have completed coursework in business or accounting. Some schools provide work-study opportunities in cooperation with local businesses. Many employers provide on-the-job training for new hires. A beginning bookkeeper may start out as a clerk performing basic tasks and gradually take on more responsibilities. Additional education and certification can improve chances for advancement. A bookkeeper can become a certified bookkeeper, a designation offered by the American Institute of Professional Bookkeepers, by completing two years of work in the field and passing an exam.

Accounting clerks and auditing clerks perform some of the same types of duties as bookkeepers. Accounting clerks generally work for large corporations. They focus on a narrow range of tasks such as entering transaction details or adding up and balancing accounts payable or accounts receivable. Auditing clerks check the accuracy of figures in financial documents.

Cost Estimator

Cost estimators collect and analyze data in order to estimate how much it will cost to manufacture a product. They take into account the time, expenses, materials, equipment, and labor involved in production. Cost estimators prepare estimates for products and services of all kinds, ranging from automobiles or computer software to government programs or infrastructure projects. They present their estimates to managers or investors, who use the findings to make decisions on whether to manufacture a potentially profitable product, begin a construction project, or make a bid on a job.

A cost estimator must possess considerable technical expertise in his or her area. The cost estimator may visit work sites and review documents such as blueprints. He or she consults with architects, engineers, and contractors involved with the project. Cost estimators also make recommendations on ways to make the product or service turn a profit, such as by reducing expenses for materials or adjusting a schedule. They may also offer suggestions on cutting expenses for existing products. Most cost estimators specialize in either construction costs or manufacturing costs.

Cost estimators may work directly for a construction company or for contractors, architectural firms, or engineering firms. At times, they may have to visit the site of a project.

Cost estimators must be proficient in the mathematics of finance as well as the technical applications relevant to their area of specialization. They must have strong analytical and computer skills and knowledge of administrative procedures. Their workday might include a visit to a factory floor as well as time spent on a computer analyzing project details and preparing cost statements.

A job as a cost estimator requires a background that includes both finance and expertise in the employer's area of work. A qualified candidate may have a bachelor's degree in accounting, business, statistics, economics, mathematics, engineering, physical sciences, or construction management. Employers often prefer candidates with hands-on experience in construction or manufacturing. Cost estimators breaking into the job should consider taking on internships or a part-time job working alongside an experienced cost estimator. Most new hires undergo an extensive on-the-job training period, since companies tend to have their own system for estimating costs. Professional associations offer a variety of certifications available to cost estimators.

Financial Analyst

Financial analysts, also called investment analysts or security analysts, provide advice on financial deals, especially buying and selling investments such as stocks and bonds. They also examine moves such as mergers and corporate takeovers.

Financial analysts study prospective investment opportunities and make recommendations based on their evaluations. When financial analysts research companies in which their clients may wish to invest, they examine financial statements and other data in order to make a projection about future performance. Financial analysts meet with representatives from the firms, discuss the prospective deal with colleagues, write reports laying out their conclusions, and recommend a plan of action to their clients. Financial analysts may make presentations to investors, staff members of their company, and the public.

In addition to examining specific investment opportunities, financial analysts must stay abreast of current economic developments, changes in laws

Networking is essential for financial analysts, who work long hours and are expected to socialize with other professionals in the field during their time off.

and regulations, financial market news, and trends in the industry. Financial instruments are growing more diverse and complex, and the field of finance is becoming more globalized. Many financial analysts specialize in a particular area. They may work for either buy-side or sell-side investment banks and other institutions. They may focus on investments in a specific economic sector or specialize in deals in a particular geographic region.

Financial analysis is a competitive field that requires hard work, long hours, and ambition. Nearly half of all financial analysts work for insurance or finance industries. Financial analysts generally hold a bachelor's and sometimes a master's degree in business administration, finance, economics, accounting, or other finance-relevant majors. Certification, such as the certified financial analyst designation, is also recommended.

Good communication skills are essential, since networking, marketing, and client service are important aspects of the field. A job in financial analysis is likely to require frequent travel to visit companies, attend conferences, and meet with potential investors. Junior analysts start out crunching data and gaining expertise, while senior analysts spend more time interacting with clients and making investment decisions. Mentorship from an experienced colleague is important for a young analyst starting out in the job.

A related career is that of personal financial adviser, or financial planner. Rather than recommending investments for an institution, personal financial advisers help individuals manage their money. Their responsibilities go beyond analyzing and making recommendations on investments. Financial advisers consider a client's overall finances and personal objectives. In addition to investments, financial advisers

THE "QUANTS" OF WALL STREET

Wall Street is the financial heart of New York City and one of the financial centers of the world. To many Americans, Wall Street symbolizes the interests of big financial firms and, in particular, the wheeling and dealing that takes place on the floor of the New York Stock Exchange. In the past, Wall Street traders were typically savvy financial insiders with degrees in business. Advanced technology and fast, high-powered computers, however, have changed the landscape of trading.

Today's financial mavericks are quantitative analysts, or "quants," who analyze financial data using complex mathematical algorithms and statistical models. Many have backgrounds in computer science, engineering, physics, or advanced mathematics rather than finance or business. Quants develop new tools for pricing, trading, and assessing the risks of financial products. As financial transactions grow faster and more complex, the demand for these mathematical savants is increasing.

Not everybody is enthusiastic about the rise of these technological wizards. Some old-style traders resent the newcomers, who don't fit into the traditional corporate culture. More relevant are questions and concerns regarding the impact of the new tools and methods of trading. Quants developed the failed formulas and instruments for assessing financial risk that contributed to the financial meltdown of 2008. More recently, some experts have expressed concerns about the risks of high-frequency trading enabled by computers, which involves massive numbers of trades over extremely short periods of times. A single glitch or error proves costly—into the hundreds of millions of dollars—when automated trades have to be halted. Despite these reservations, quants provide essential services in modern-day Wall Street, and their expertise will only become more indispensable in an increasingly technological financial world.

manage insurance coverage, retirement planning, tax returns, and the financial impact of life decisions such as marriage or returning to school. They may also consult other professionals involved in a client's financial affairs, such as attorneys, accountants, and investment bankers.

Another career related to financial analysis is that of budget analyst. Budget analysts organize the finances of institutions. They track spending and make recommendations concerning budget proposals for future needs. Budget analysts play an important role in overseeing financial resources for government agencies, schools, and corporations.

Financial Manager

Financial managers are responsible for handling the finances of a corporation or other organization. This includes decisions regarding investments, accounting, banking, insurance, and securities. Financial managers work with top executives to set financial goals and supervise employees who handle the company's finances. They prepare financial statements, cash-flow reports, and profit forecasts. A financial manager used to devote a great deal of time to tracking financial data. Today, with computers organizing such information, financial managers concentrate more on analyzing financial statistics. They may look for ways to raise funds, cut costs, and take advantage of market trends.

Financial managers must take care to comply with the complex maze of laws and regulations relevant to their company. They should also be experts on the processes and challenges specific to their industry.

The term "financial manager" includes a range of more specific occupations. The BLS *Occupational Outlook Handbook* describes six examples of financial manager job titles. A controller is generally a high-level position at a large corporation. The controller's duties may include setting financial strategies, preparing reports on the organization's financial condition, managing the payroll system, and overseeing the accounting, audit, and budget departments. A treasurer or finance officer oversees the financial administration of an organization. The treasurer must handle responsibilities such as investing or borrowing so as to minimize financial risk that could cause the company to lose value. A credit manager oversees a company's credit department, which is involved in collecting payments and implementing credit policies. A cash manager handles a company's cash. The cash manager conducts collections and short-term investments, monitoring cash flow in order to meet the company's needs and obligations.

A family meets with a financial adviser. Financial advisers help clients meet their financial goals, which sometimes means that clients must evaluate their financial situation and make tough decisions.

A risk manager is charged with minimizing a company's risk caused by financial uncertainty in making

investments. An insurance manager makes decisions on whether or not to obtain insurance against specific risks that could lead to losses.

Financial managing can be a high-pressure job that requires putting in long hours of work, meeting tight deadlines, and analyzing financial products that are becoming increasingly more complex. About 30 percent of financial managers work in the fields of finance or insurance.

A financial manager generally starts out by earning a bachelor's degree in business administration, finance, economics, or accounting. Some financial managers seek certification, such as the certified financial analyst (CFA) or certified public accountant (CPA) designation. Many also pursue a master's degree and additional specialized training—because of the constant new developments in the field, lifelong learning is necessary to keep up. A financial manager typically begins in a lower-level position, such as financial analyst or accountant, and gradually earns promotions and increased responsibilities.

Actuary

Actuaries are business professionals who use statistics to estimate the financial consequences of risk. They apply mathematical and statistical models to determine the probability that certain events will occur in the future. Insurance companies use actuaries' findings to set rates and prepare for future claims from customers collecting on their policies.

Actuaries assess risks of all kinds. They predict the likelihood of automobile accidents, hurricanes, theft, and other events that lead to loss of property. Much actuarial work focuses on health and life insurance. Actuaries compile and analyze demographic statistics such as rates of births, deaths, and marriage. From this information, they create computer models that forecast the likelihood and costs of events such as illness, accident, or death. They may construct actuarial tables, which list the probability of death for people of any age. For example, according to a recent Social Security actuarial table, a fifteen-year-old boy had a death probability of 0.000456 and a life expectancy of 61.62 more years (for a total of 76.62 years). A fifteen-year-old girl had a death probability of 0.000229 and a life expectancy of 66.44 more years (for a total of 81.44 years).

Insurance companies use actuarial statistics to determine rates for life insurance, health insurance, automobile insurance, property insurance, liability in-

THE ACTUARIAL EXAM: DO YOU HAVE WHAT IT TAKES?

Actuaries must pass either four or six exams—depending on the licensing society—to be certified as an associate actuary. Further exams qualify an actuary as a fellow. Here are some sample questions from the preliminary exams:

1. An auto insurance company has 10,000 policyholders. Each policyholder is classified as
   i young or old;
   ii male or female; and
   iii married or single.
Of these policyholders, 3,000 are young, 4,600 are male, and 7,000 are married. The policyholders can also be classified as 1,320 young males, 3,010 married males, and 1,400 young married persons. Finally, 600 of the policyholders are young married males.

How many of the company's policyholders are young, female, and single?
   a 280
   b 423
   c 486
   d 880
   e 896

2. An insurer offers a health plan to the employees of a large company. As part of this plan, the individual employees may choose exactly two of the supplementary coverages A, B, and C, or they may choose no supplementary coverage. The proportions of the company's

employees that choose coverages A, B, and C are 1/4, 1/3, and 5/12 respectively.

Determine the probability that a randomly chosen employee will choose no supplementary coverage.

a 0

b 47/144

c ½

d 97/144

e 7/9

3. A tour operator has a bus that can accommodate 20 tourists. The operator knows that tourists may not show up, so he sells 21 tickets. The probability that an individual tourist will not show up is 0.02, independent of all other tourists. Each ticket costs $50 and is non-refundable if a tourist fails to show up. If a tourist shows up and a seat is not available, the tour operator has to pay $100 (ticket cost + $50 penalty) to the tourist. What is the expected revenue of the tour operator?

a $935

b $950

c $967

d $976

e $985

Answers: 1 – d; 2 – c; 3 – e

Source: http://www.beanactuary.org/how/is/?fa=sample-actuarial-problems

surance, and unemployment insurance. They aim to set policy rates at a level where the company will be able to afford to pay out claims and still make a profit. Actuaries also design insurance policies and other business strategies related to risk.

Most actuaries are employed by insurance companies, although they also work for corporations and for the government. But the need for their expertise is expanding. Demand for actuaries is increasing in a range of companies that deal with financial risk.

The career path to becoming a certified actuary is long and challenging. Many actuaries show an early interest in math and excel in school. An actuary typically earns a degree in mathematics, statistics, business, or actuarial science. In order to become a fully certified actuary, a candidate must take a series of at least seven difficult exams—which include topics from several branches of advanced mathematics—that take up to ten years to complete. Actuaries are accredited by the Casualty Actuarial Society (CAS) or the Society of Actuaries (SOA). Many students begin taking the first exams while still in college. Some companies hire candidates who have passed two of the exams and therefore have proven their dedication to the field. The employer will pay the exam fees and give new hires paid time to study. Pay rises as the candidate successfully completes exams.

According to BeAnActuary.org, candidates generally study one hundred hours for each hour of exam time—and many of the exams last multiple hours. The site suggests completing internships relating to both property/casualty and life and health in order to decide which aspect of actuarial science is the best fit. It also points out that actuaries perform a valuable service that most people never consider: "We are the analytical backbone of our society's financial security programs. We are the brains behind the financial safeguards in our personal lives, so we can go about our day without worrying too much about what the future may hold for us."

Insurance Underwriter

Insurance underwriters review applications for insurance and decide whether or not to offer coverage, and at what price. They act as middlemen between the insurance agents who sell insurance and the insurance companies that issue policies.

An underwriter determines the potential financial risk associated with insuring an individual or company. An underwriter's responsibilities don't overlap with those of an actuary—the underwriter rates an application using guidelines and tables set by an actuary. Nonetheless, the underwriter does have to use good judgment; they don't merely enter data into computer programs. Underwriters assess the recommendations returned by the computer when making a decision on whether or not to offer coverage.

The underwriter must carefully weigh the risks for each application. If an underwriter is too cautious and rejects too many applications, the company will lose business. If the underwriter approves too many risky applications, the company will lose money paying out claims. In addition, the underwriter must determine the optimum price for each policy and the extent of coverage that will turn a healthy profit.

As in the case of actuaries, underwriters tend to specialize in property/casualty or life and health insurance. In addition, some underwriters evaluate applications for mortgages. A different range of risks are assessed for each category. An underwriter evaluating an application for automobile insurance will examine the applicant's driving record, while an underwriter for a health insurance policy will consider medical records. In some cases, an underwriter may request additional documents such as credit reports or background checks. The job may require travel, such as when an applicant wants to insure a piece of property and the underwriter decides to examine it in person.

Most underwriters hold a bachelor's degree in business or accounting. Several underwriting associations offer various types of professional certification. Underwriters generally start out in their career by working under the supervision of a more experienced colleague. A master's degree will increase an underwriter's chances of advancing to senior and management positions.

Loan Officer

Loan officers advise, evaluate, and decide whether or not to recommend approval of loan applications for people and businesses. Loan officers act as the public face of their financial institution in advising and soliciting clients. They are charged with matching clients with the best loan for their needs, but they also must evaluate whether or not the client is likely to be able to repay the loan.

A loan officer begins the process of granting a loan by meeting with the client, who could be an individual making a purchase or a representative of a business looking to expand. Loan officers also oversee loan modifications, such as consolidating several loans. During the initial meetings, a loan officer explains options, obtains information, answers questions, and begins guiding the clients through the process. Once the client has submitted an application, the loan officer

Loan officers often meet with customers at car dealerships and other locations. Loan officers must have great interpersonal skills as well as solid business-related math skills.

reviews financial documentation such as income, tax files, and credit reports in order to determine whether the prospective borrower is credit-worthy. If the application is approved, the loan officer will arrange a payment schedule.

Loan officers work for financial institutions of all types and sizes, including commercial banks, credit unions, and mortgage companies. They also work out of car dealerships. Most loan officers specialize in commercial loans to businesses, consumer loans to individuals, and mortgages on real estate. Financial institutions hire loan underwriters, who specialize in evaluating loan applications for approval, and loan collection officers, who work with clients who fail to make payments on their loan.

Loan officers must have a solid grasp of statistics as well as good judgment in deciding whether or not a borrower should qualify for a loan. Excellent communication skills are essential, since a loan officer must put clients at ease during a process that can sometimes be tense and frustrating. Good customer service skills are also important, since loan officers often seek out prospective clients.

Most employers look for candidates who have a bachelor's degree in finance, business, or economics. They learn through on-the-job training, although some loan officers begin in lower level positions and work their way up through advancement and continuing education. Loan officers specializing in mortgages must hold a mortgage loan originator license. Certification of various types is available for loan officers.

Economist

Economics is the field involved with the production and allocation of resources, goods, and services in society. You might be surprised to see no mention of money in the definition. Economics is considered a social science, and economists examine topics such as supply and demand, the decisions of individual consumers, the consequences of government policies, and much more. They develop new theories and principles based on their conclusions and try to forecast future economic trends and developments. In practice, the field of economics requires a solid understanding of statistics and mathematics.

Economists perform research in a wide variety of areas. They may concentrate on issues such as international trade, government spending, unemployment levels, taxation, prices, interest rates, the banking system, and monetary policy. They may evaluate the economic forces affecting health care, education, and the environment. Economists examine data and statistics—some economists develop methods for collecting information for surveys—and analyze them using mathematical and statistical models. They describe their findings in reports, charts, and presentations. Often, the results involve a forecast or recommendation that will be used in making future plans, policies, and decisions.

Most economists specialize in a particular subfield. Microeconomists study the economic decisions of individuals and companies and their effect on prices. Macroeconomists and monetary economists study

overall economic activity, which includes the total con-
sumption of products by businesses and individuals.
They may focus on interest rates, overall price levels,
unemployment rates, and economic growth.

International economists study international trade,
globalization, and exchange rates. Financial economists study the processes of saving, investing, and
dealing with risk, as well as financial markets and institutions. Public finance economists study the government's role in the economy, examining both programs
and policies as well as the political process. Labor
economists study the supply and demand of workers
and employers and examine issues such as wage and
employment levels. Industrial organization economists study how markets, competition, prices, and
antitrust policies affect companies within an industry.
Econometricians use mathematical models and analysis to measure economic phenomena. Mathematical
economists develop mathematical tools and use game
theory—the analysis of how people make decisions—
to answer economic questions.

Economists also specialize in areas related to
health, education, welfare, law, business administration, accounting, agriculture, the environment, and urban, rural, and regional economics. Some economists
study economic history, economic systems, economic
development, technical change, and growth.

Over half of all economists work for the government at the federal, state, or local level. They collect
and analyze data for numerous departments and agencies within the government, from the Department of
Labor to the National Bureau of Economic Research.

Government economists release facts, figures, and statistics about the health of the economy, such as the gross domestic product (GDP), corporate profits, personal income and spending, unemployment rates, and personal saving. They also forecast the economic consequences of laws, policies, and regulations.

Some economists work for large corporations. They analyze factors that affect the industry, such as demand, competition, and market conditions. Other economists make analyses and forecasts for consulting services, research firms, and think tanks. Economists also teach and conduct research at universities.

A master's degree or a Ph.D. is required for most jobs in the field of economics. A candidate with a bachelor's degree in economics may find an entry-level government job related to collecting data or preparing reports under the supervision of a higher-level economist. Internships can supply valuable work experience.

CHAPTER FOUR

Conjectures, Solutions, and Codes

Careers in Theoretical Mathematics, Operations Analysis, and Cryptanalysis

Mathematics is a valuable tool in a variety of spheres, including finance, the natural sciences, engineering, computer science, and many others. But although applied math concepts are important in these fields, they are part of a larger toolkit of knowledge and skills. A much smaller number of disciplines require use of mathematics as the primary skill or the focus of one's career.

Math careers can range widely from high-level theoretical and academic work to elementary math education. Theoretical mathematicians expand the theoretical limits of mathematics through research, while applied mathematicians seek practical uses for mathematic principles in the real world. Two careers that require applied use of advanced mathematics are operations research analyst and cryptanalyst. Operations research analysts use math to improve the efficiency of operations carried out by large organizations, from military maneuvers to the introduction of a new product on the market. Cryptanalysts crack codes and design new security measures for information systems. At the other end of the spectrum, math teachers share their expertise with students who range from youngsters learning to count to adult graduate students embarking on their own high-level research.

Many people with degrees in math love their jobs. They enjoy the sense of accomplishment that comes with meeting mathematical challenges and report a high level of satisfaction in their work.

Mathematician

Mathematicians use higher mathematics and technology to solve problems. Theoretical mathematicians concentrate on developing new mathematical theories and finding relationships between existing mathematical principles. Applied mathematicians use math to solve practical problems in many fields, which range from science to finance to urban planning. The two categories of mathematicians frequently overlap. The principles conceived by theoretical mathematicians have real-world uses in engineering, data analysis, and many other applications. Applied mathematicians draw on mathematical theories in their everyday work.

The renowned theoretical mathematician William P. Thurston, for example, conceived of the Geometrization Conjecture. He showed that all possible three-dimensional spaces are made up of eight different geometric structures. Thurston pursued theoretical

Mathematician William P. Thurston, 1982 winner of the prestigious Fields Medal, was best known for his work in geometry and topology, a branch of mathematics that examines shapes and spaces.

mathematics for its own sake, not for possible applications. Nonetheless, his work has been used by cosmologists trying to determine the shape of the universe.

Theoretical mathematicians relish the intellectual challenge of the field. To a theoretical mathematician, there are always new problems to tackle on the horizon. In his book *Letters to a Young Mathematician*, mathematics professor and writer Ian Stewart comments, "It always astonishes me that so many people seem to believe that mathematics is limited to what they were taught at school, so basically 'it's all been done.' Even more astonishing is the assumption that because 'the answers are all in the back of the book,' there is no scope for creativity, and no questions remain unanswered." Theoretical mathematicians seek to expand understanding of mathematics by developing new theorems, principles, patterns, and even new branches of mathematics.

Most theoretical mathematicians are employed in academia, teaching at colleges and universities or doing work at research institutes. They often specialize in one or more advanced areas of mathematics, such as logic, set theory, abstract algebra, discrete mathematics, number theory, geometry, topology, dynamical systems, combinatorics, stochastic processes, graph theory, game theory, probability, or statistics. They use computers to process data, create models, and run simulations.

Mathematicians who work in universities and colleges teach classes, serve as advisers to students, supervise graduate student research, and collaborate with colleagues. They also attend to administrative duties, such as writing research grants, serving on committees, and holding office hours. In order to keep up with the developments in the field, mathematicians read professional journals, consult with colleagues, and travel to conferences.

Mathematics can be a solitary pursuit, but much research is collaborative. Young mathematicians and graduate students can gain experience by working as a junior member of a team. Later, they can pursue their own research as a leader of a team.

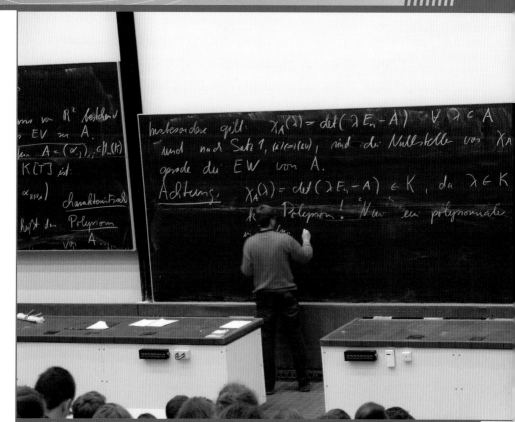

A mathematics professor in a lecture hall writes out equations.
Many theoretical mathematicians are affiliated with universities or
colleges, where they teach as well as carry out research.

The field of mathematics has been growing increasingly interdisciplinary. Researchers work with scientists, engineers, and mathematicians from other specializations on projects that require expertise in a number of fields. Ian Stewart describes working on a project involving over thirty researchers, including various mathematicians, engineers, and programmers. The names of nine authors appeared on the final paper.

A Ph.D. is generally required for a career as a theoretical mathematician. It usually takes at least five years to earn a doctorate. The job market is highly competitive, and a graduate student should start thinking about a job search before completing a degree. Prospective employers are impressed by the grants and awards a job candidate has received and his or her teaching experience, volunteer work, and participation in activities such as conferences and seminars. A job application packet often requires a research statement and a statement of teaching philosophy. In such a competitive field, many graduate students may say that they'll take any job they can get, but prospective employers are likely to be more impressed with candidates who have a clear idea of their focus, interests, and goals.

Operations Research Analyst

Operations research analysts apply mathematics to situations and problems in the everyday operations of large organizations that require significant coordination. The analysts' work can inform management decisions in areas such as scheduling, marketing, product development, inventory control, organizational structure, queueing (such as directing ticket or exhibit lines at a museum), environmental sustainability, and optimizing (such as improved product design or the achievement of better search engine algorithms and results). Operations research analysts work in manufacturing, transportation systems, finance, the government (especially the military), health care, telecommunications, private consulting firms, engineering services, and many other areas.

Operations research is an interdisciplinary pursuit that also draws on engineering, logic, psychology, management principles, and other social and political sciences. It is closely related to management science (the field devoted to improving an organization's decision

An operations research analyst visits a workplace. Operations research analysts will consider information from a variety of sources, including input from workers, when running advanced computer models.

making and efficiency) and to analytics (the utilization of data in making decisions).

An operations research analyst begins a project by defining the problem, based on the management's goals and objectives. How should an airline schedule landings at an airport? What quantities of equipment and raw materials should a company buy for manufacturing a product? The operations research analyst then collects data, talking to people involved in the issues being examined and gathering facts and figures. He or she then analyzes and interprets the data using a variety of advanced statistical and analytical methods, such as mathematical models, simulations, and optimizations. Changing the values of variables in the equations yields different possible real-world outcomes. Most of the operations research analyst's work is done on the computer, and the operations research analyst may have to write new computer programs specific to the project. Once the operations research analyst has devised a solution to the problem, he or she presents recommendations to managers and executives.

Operations research had its origins in military planning efforts during World War II. After the war ended, the principles of operations research began to spread to industry, business, and organizations in other fields. Operations research remains crucial to defense efforts—many operations research analysts work for the government or for consulting firms that offer services to defense agencies. The Military Operations Research Society (MORS), a professional organization of military operations research experts, addresses national security issues for numerous branches of the government. Operations research analysts also work in professional, scientific, and technical services, in finance and insurance, and in manufacturing. Telecommunication services is a fast growing area of the field.

Anyone interested in pursuing a career in operations research should have a keen interest in finding practical solutions to complicated problems. This requires creative thinking as well as analytical and reasoning skills. Candidates with a bachelor's degree in a major such as mathematics, business, or engineering are qualified for entry level jobs in operations research. Students should take classes in statistics, probability, calculus, linear algebra, economics, and computer science. Many schools offer only a graduate-level degree in operations research, and a master's degree or Ph.D. is recommended in order to advance in the field.

Cryptanalyst

Cryptanalysis is the art and science of decoding encrypted information concealed in codes and ciphers. Throughout history, cryptographers—code writers—have hidden messages through various encryption techniques. Cryptanalysts—code breakers—have tried to decipher them. One of the most famous uses of codes in recent history occurred during World War II, when Navajo Native Americans encoded messages using a system based on their native language. Japanese cryptanalysts were never able to break the code. Today, in an increasingly high-tech, data-driven world, cryptanalysts are more in demand than ever before. Many work in telecommunications and information technology designing new methods of encryption and making systems more secure against hackers. ("Cryptanalyst" is the general job title that describes work in encrypting information as well as in deciphering codes. The terms "cryptographer" and "cryptologist" are also accurate, but they are less frequently used.)

Information can be encrypted using many different systems, such as by replacing a word or group of words with another word, number, or symbol. Today, digital information is encrypted using complex cryptographic systems. Modern code breakers use encryption algorithms that involve advanced applications of mathematics and computer science. The process of breaking a code is a combination of high-tech techniques, trial and error, persistence, and sometimes luck.

Cryptanalysts work in every sector that requires information security—for many organizations, the theft of vital data can be even more detrimental than a physical theft. Cryptanalysts are employed by many military and government agencies. Cryptanalysts with the Federal Bureau of Investigations (FBI), for example, may decrypt communications from terrorists, foreign intelligence agents (spies), and criminals. The National Security Agency (NSA) also employs many cryptanalysts and offers a three-year on-the-job training program as well as opportunities for college study. Other employers include telecommunications companies, law enforcement agencies, financial institutions, and consulting firms.

Cryptanalysts design algorithms and encryption systems to make their information infrastructure—

whether it's a financial transaction system or a database of trade secrets—more secure. They also work as research scientists for universities and private institutions. As hackers and foreign agents develop more sophisticated methods of illicitly retrieving information, cryptanalysts must continually devise new methods of securing data.

Anybody interested in becoming a cryptanalyst should have a lively and curious mind as well as formidable mathematical and analytical skills. According to a government job description on the career site Monster.com, "Cryptanalysts typically possess knowledge of geography, English, history and archeology, philosophy and theology, foreign language, mathematics, and computers and electronics. General skill areas include speaking, critical thinking, active learning, social perceptiveness, reading comprehension, writing, complex problem solving, and mathematics."

Expertise and ingenuity, rather than any specific educational background, is the key to a successful career as a cryptanalyst. In practice, however, most cryptanalysts hold bachelor's degrees and often advanced degrees in mathematics or computer science. Continuing education is absolutely essential because of the fast pace of innovation in the world of information security.

Math Teacher

If you're a high school student, your math teacher probably represents the public face of the subject to you. Some math teachers possess a combination of passion and dedication for the job that can spark a lifelong interest in mathematics in their students. In a numbers-driven society and economy that rewards mathematical aptitude, it's crucial that schools encourage math teachers who can transform students into capable young mathematicians who love the subject.

Math teachers must be excited not just about the subject of math but about sharing math with their students. In *Letters to a Young Mathematician*, Ian Stewart states, "To my mind, the most important feature of good teachers is that they put themselves in the student's position... Whether you are delivering a lecture or talking with students during office hours, you have to remember that what

A math teacher helps out students working on a group project. Out-standing math teachers can engage students' curiosity and inspire an appreciation of mathematics and its applications in other disciplines.

seems perfectly obvious and transparent to you may be mysterious and opaque to someone who had not encountered the ideas before." Math teachers must convey concepts in terms that students will understand, and they must recognize when students are struggling.

Math is taught at every educational level, including elementary school, middle school, high school, community colleges, four-year colleges, and universities. At each of these levels, the material is highly structured. Teachers may be required to meet certain core curriculum standards for each grade or class. They must prepare students for standardized tests and meet college entrance requirements. In college courses, the broad course content may be decided by the entire math faculty, and professors prepare a syllabus describing the week-by-week details.

Teachers give lectures, hold discussions, supervise classroom work, and maintain discipline. Some teachers include innovative teaching methods using technology or invite guest speakers to address the students. Behind the scenes, they grade papers, plan lessons, score tests, keep records, and perform administrative tasks. They may draft assignments, quizzes, and exams. Math teachers hold conferences with parents and consult with colleagues and administrators. They may act as sponsors for extracurricular activities, either associated with math or involving an unrelated interest. Teachers may attend workshops or conferences.

Math teachers must hold at least a bachelor's degree. Elementary teachers may major in education,

TEACH FOR AMERICA

Teach for America is a nonprofit organization that plac-
es recent college graduates in teaching positions in low-
income, rural, or otherwise underserved communities.
The new teachers undergo an intensive five-week training program in the summer before they begin teaching.
They generally receive "alternative" certification at the
end—procedures vary from one state to another—and
earn full certification during their teaching stint. Some
teachers even go on to earn master's degrees by the
end of their two-year commitment period. Some Teach
for America teachers continue to work in education after
their two years are over. Others go on to other pursuits,
but they forever carry with them an awareness of the
value of universal quality education. Teach for America
includes an initiative to encourage graduates in STEM
areas to take up teaching.

Many Teach for America alumni have gone on to
prestigious careers in education. One such individual
is Jason Kamras, who, in 1996, became a math teacher
in Washington, D.C., for Teach for America after earning a bachelor's degree in public policy from Princeton
University. He returned to school to earn a master's
degree in education from Harvard in 1999. In 2002,
Kamras piloted a redesigned math curriculum that re-
duced the number of students receiving "below basic"
test scores from 80 percent to 40 percent. In 2005,
he was honored as National Teacher of the Year in a
White House ceremony. Today, Kamras works as Chief
of Human Capital for the District of Columbia Public
Schools (DCPS), ensuring that Washington, D.C., students are taught by the best teachers possible.

Jason Kamras, a math teacher who believes that all students deserve a quality education regardless of income, speaks after receiving the 2005 National Teacher of the Year Award.

while high school teachers are more likely to major in mathematics. All teachers in public schools must obtain and maintain certification. Requirements for certification vary from one state to another. Some states require student teaching or the completion of certain classes in education. Teachers just starting out on the job are sometimes mentored by experienced teachers. Continuing education courses may be required to retain certification, and a master's degree opens up more career advancement opportunities.

Professors teaching at colleges or universities must hold advanced degrees. A new instructor may start out as an assistant professor and work his or her way up the ladder to associate professor and full professor. In many colleges and universities, original research and publication credits are crucial for advancement and gaining tenure.

CHAPTER FIVE

From Your First Job to a Lifetime of Learning

A degree related to mathematics opens up worlds of professional opportunities. Job openings in STEM areas are projected to increase at rates significantly above those of average occupations through 2020. In the data-driven twenty first century, employers are becoming more interested in hiring math-savvy employees. Opportunities for math majors exist in diverse areas from finance to science to teaching. And graduates with math degrees generally don't have regrets about their choice of field—they tend to report high levels of satisfaction in their careers.

Starting out in the work world is not easy, however, even in high demand career areas. Getting a first job can be tough. The transition to the workplace can be jarring. But a solid career strategy can lead to a successful job hunt and a satisfying first job. The process requires clear goals, good organization, savvy networking, and confidence in conveying one's professional abilities to prospective employers.

Career Resources

A first-time job seeker should draw on a wide range of resources for help in researching positions, getting organized for a job search, and preparing for life after graduation. Take advantage of the services and opportunities offered by your college or university. Career resource centers provide practical job search assistance of all types, from résumé critiques and job databases to workshops on professional attire. Your academic department will provide you with job openings posted by employers in your field. Attend any career fairs sponsored by your college.

Talk to your academic adviser and your professors—they may be able to tell you about available research or teaching positions. They may also be able to give you relevant advice based on their own career experience, such as how to hone your research statement for job application packets or how best to articulate a teaching philosophy. Before you leave campus, arrange for letters of recommendation and references that you can list on your résumé and job applications. Solid references include people who can vouch for your abilities and qualifications, such as former professors and employers. Family and friends are not appropriate as references.

Check out job postings from a variety of sources. Scan the listings in newspapers and periodicals,

Career resource centers offer valuable resources for students charting their career paths. Here, students visit Temple University's career center in Philadelphia, Pennsylvania, during an event for freshmen.

especially publications specializing in your field of interest. Check out online job sites and the career sections on the Web sites of professional societies. The American Mathematics Society, for example, provides extensive career information on the current job market, job openings, internships, and fellowships. It also offers advice about launching a career in the field. Many

companies and organizations have an employment section on their Web sites, and federal government jobs are listed at USAJobs.gov. Read job descriptions to find positions that match your qualifications, rather than just scanning job titles.

Making a Great First Impression

Before you shake hands with a prospective employer at a job interview, he or she will already have a broad idea of your work and educational history. Your résumé presents your accomplishments to potential employers before they ever meet you. Specifications for job application materials tend to vary, but they all require a résumé, which is a document that summarizes your professional qualifications. In addition to education and work experience, it also lists relevant information such as activities, awards, credentials, interests, or skills that might be pertinent to the job.

There are many different formats for résumés, and you will need to research which is most appropriate for your background, objectives, and career field or industry. All résumés include your educational background and your work experience. Additional categories may include activities, honors, certifications,

The internet offers a variety of resources for job seekers, from general job search services to professional associations offering tips for advancing in a particular field.

and references. When possible, you should tailor your résumé to the position for which you're applying. As you're drafting your résumé, consult career Web sites and references, and ask a career counselor at your school for tips.

Once you've landed a job interview, you need to begin preparing well in advance. You'll need to consider the substance of the interview—how you're going to present your qualifications—as well as practical considerations, such as what you're going to wear and

CRAFTING A GREAT COVER LETTER

When you're sending out a job application packet, pay attention to the employer's specifications. If the job posting asked for two writing samples, don't send four. Don't miss the employer's deadline date. And don't neglect to craft a cover letter with details tailored to the specific job description.

If you're looking for your first job, you may be sending out reams of applications to a variety of different types of employers. The cover letter is your opportunity to introduce yourself to a prospective employer. You need to convince the person reading the letter not just that you're a good mathematician, but that you're a great candidate for the specific position for which you're applying.

You should send a cover letter with every job application unless the employer specifies "no cover letters." A cover letter should not repeat the exact same list of details that you list in your résumé, although you may want to emphasize a few of your key qualifications or accomplishments. Your cover letter should demonstrate your written communication skills and convey a sense of your personality, although you must maintain a professional tone.

A few tips: Keep your cover letter short. Your employer may be reading dozens for the position, and he or she won't have the time or patience for long letters. Show that you possess some knowledge about the company and have done some research. Finally, don't be afraid to sell yourself. Employers are looking for confident candidates who can express why they're a great match for the job.

how much commute time you'll need to allot in the morning. Remember that you'll need to emphasize a different skill set if you're interviewing for a teaching position, for example, than you will for a research job. Learn everything you can about the company or organization ahead of time so that you'll be able to describe why you'd be able to fulfill the job requirements.

The interview is basically a conversation between you and the interviewer, so determine beforehand what you most want to convey during the exchange. Your goals for the interview—in addition to

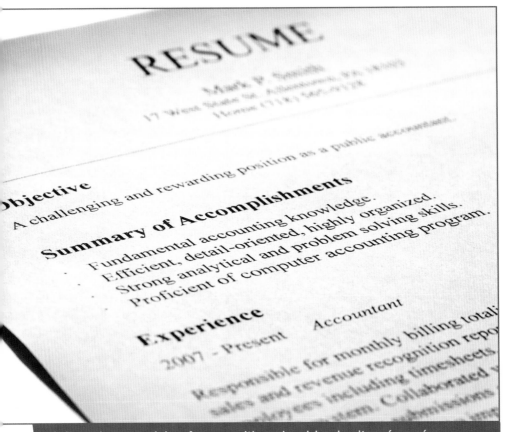

Job seekers applying for a position should submit a résumé or a curriculum vitae (CV), which includes a longer summary of educational background and professional experience than a résumé.

landing the job—may include aspects of your interview performance. For example, you may focus upon presenting a confident, positive attitude. Or you may try to ensure that you discuss specific points that illustrate your qualifications and mention specific accomplishments relevant to the job requirements. Everybody feels nervous before a job interview, but walking in well-prepared, with a clear strategy and set of goals, will improve your chances of making a good impression.

Working Your Network

Networking is a valuable strategy at every point in your career. Your network includes professional connections in your field. People in your network may be able to inform you about jobs that aren't advertised publicly. They may make calls on your behalf and give you information and advice. You gain network connections through deliberate introductions as well as by chance or professional connections, such as by becoming acquainted with colleagues at a conference. Many of the members of your network will be happy to support you in a job search or referral, and you may be able to reciprocate at a later point.

New workers just starting out in the job market often benefit from the support of a mentor. A mentor is an experienced professional who can listen to your concerns and offer guidance. He or she can also help you with networking and navigating the unfamiliar terrain of the field. You may consider your mentor a friend, but the relationship is often more formal and

A job candidate should demonstrate a positive attitude during a job interview in order to convince the prospective employer that he or she would be a good person to work with on a day-to-day basis.

respectful than friendship with peers. On the other hand, some people are able to find mentors within their own families or social circle. You might seek out a mentor

through your job, professional association, programs at your college, volunteer work, or mutual acquaintances.

Early in your career, your network begins with your professors, advisers, mentors, fellow alumni, and former employers. Family, friends, and acquaintances from extracurricular activities or volunteer work may be able to give you a hand as well. You'll need to actively seek out fellow networkers by making a point to meet new people and being ready to hand out networking materials such as a business card or a brochure if the opportunity arises. As you progress in your career, your network will include more colleagues, collaborators, and work supervisors.

Professional associations can be a valuable networking tool. When someone from your network helps you out, be sure to follow up on the tip and thank him or her afterward. Throughout the course of your career, you must develop, maintain, and constantly expand and refine your network of colleagues. You must also keep learning from and being inspired by them.

Networking can be a key to success in many fields. Today, social networking sites for professionals provide another means of connecting with business associates and potential employers.

Your First Job

A first job is a chance to prove your abilities and make connections in the field. It's also a learning experience—new hires usually start out doing low-level tasks and work their way up to assignments with more responsibilities that may be more interesting. Some jobs include a formal training period, or new employees may work under close supervision of a more experienced colleague.

This is the case with most careers related to mathematics, regardless of the specific field. Newly graduated architects spend a long internship period working for an architectural firm. Many astronomers or physicists with new Ph.D.s perform postdoctoral research under the supervision of an established scientist. A cost estimator generally receives on-the-job training from an experienced colleague. An operations research analyst will probably start out as a research assistant supervised by a senior operations research analyst. Across all fields, new employees must prove their work ethic and demonstrate their dedication and abilities before they can take on more responsibilities.

Periodically, you will receive formal and informal feedback on your job. A supervisor may congratulate you for completing a project. You will probably receive a written and oral annual performance review. Take heed of both compliments and criticism when any feedback is offered.

Advancement in your career brings more responsibilities, more independence, and better pay. Depending on the nature of your field, you may advance to senior-level employee, manager, administrator, or supervisor. Eventually, you may decide to leave the company to start up your own business.

Lifelong Learning

Most high-tech STEM fields are constantly undergoing new developments, and lifelong learning is essential for remaining up-to-date in the field. Many careers in applied mathematics also involve computer science, the natural sciences, finance, and economics. These fields tend to undergo constant transformation as computer scientists make breakthroughs, scientists announce discoveries, and economists grapple with and analyze the repercussions of new financial crises and developments. In addition, every year brings new laws, regulations, trends, and industry developments. Some professions require that members

attend formal training courses in order to maintain certification. Regardless of requirements, continuing education can bring substantial benefits in the workplace.

A first job gives young workers the opportunity to demonstrate their capabilities and learn the routines and expectations of the workplace.

Some STEM math careers require graduate-level degrees for even entry-level jobs. In other careers, master's degrees and Ph.D.s are advantageous but not absolutely necessary. Many ambitious employees holding a bachelor's degree reach a point in their career when they begin to consider the possibility of returning to school to complete a higher degree. A graduate level program may involve learning about a specialized discipline, studying the managerial aspect of the field, or making a transition to a different area of applied mathematics (for example, the American Mathematical Society offers an article on making the transition from the academic world to a career in finance).

Keeping up in the field includes pursuits other than taking formal course work and maintaining certification. Depending on your area, you may attend conferences and meetings with other members at the top of your profession. You may read journals or other publications, perform research, write articles, or serve as a mentor to new employees. A lifelong commitment to your mathematics career will lead to a stimulating and rewarding professional life in a field that is continually being transformed and enlivened by innovation.

GLOSSARY

ADMINISTRATIVE Pertaining to management of the daily operations of an organization.

ALGORITHM A step-by-step set of rules for solving a problem, especially in mathematics or computing.

ANALYTICAL Of or relating to the careful study of something; of or relating to analysis of something; having or showing skill in thinking or reasoning.

APPLY To put specialized knowledge and skills to practical use.

ASSOCIATE'S DEGREE An undergraduate degree generally awarded after two years of college study.

BACHELOR'S DEGREE An undergraduate degree obtained after completing a four-year college program.

CANDIDATE An individual under consideration for a job or other position.

CERTIFICATION The awarding of a certificate or license upon completion of a course of study or the passing of an exam.

COMPUTER SCIENCE The branch of engineering that deals with computer hardware, software, programming, and information technology; a branch of science that deals with the theory of computation or the design of computers; the study of computers, their design, and their uses for computation, data processing, and systems control, including design and development of computer hardware and software, and programming.

DATABASE An organized set of data (information) in a computer system that can be easily searched and updated.

DOCTORATE (PH.D.) The highest academic degree granted by a university.

ENGINEER A person who designs, develops, and builds things, generally specializing in a specific branch such as mechanical, electrical, or computer software engineering.

EXECUTIVE A high-level business manager.

FACULTY The body of teachers in a college or university.

GRANT An award of money, intended for a purpose such as for education or research, that does not have to be repaid.

INTERDISCIPLINARY Related to two or more fields of study.

INTERN A trainee or low-level assistant, especially one who takes employment (usually unpaid or low pay) to gain practical experience.

LICENSE Official permission from the government or other authority, such as to practice a trade.

MANAGEMENT The executives or administrators who direct and operate a business or organization.

MARKETING The process of promoting a product or service to potential buyers.

MASTER'S DEGREE An advanced degree obtained after completing a one- or two-year graduate program.

MENTOR An experienced adviser who offers professional help and counsel to a less experienced person in the field.

REFERENCE Someone providing a statement of professional qualifications on behalf of a job applicant; also, the statement itself.

RÉSUMÉ A summary of one's professional qualifications and work experience.

STATISTICS The field related to the collection, organization, analysis, and interpretation of large amounts of numerical data.

THEORETICAL Pertaining to theories or ideas rather than practical applications.

FOR MORE INFORMATION

American Mathematical Society (AMS)
201 Charles Street
Providence, RI 02904-2294
(401) 455-4000
Web site: http://www.ams.org
The AMS, founded in 1888 to further the interests of
    mathematical research and scholarship, serves the
    national and international community through its
    publications, meetings, advocacy, and programs.

American Statistical Association (ASA)
732 North Washington Street
Alexandria, VA 22314-1943
(703) 684-1221
Web site: http://amstat.org
The world's largest community of statisticians, ASA
    members serve in industry, government, and aca-
    demia in more than ninety countries, advancing re-
    search and promoting sound statistical practice to
    inform public policy and improve human welfare.

Association for Women in Mathematics (AWM)
11240 Waples Mill Road
Suite 200
Fairfax, VA 22030
(703) 934-0163
https://sites.google.com/site/awmmath
The purpose of the AWM is to encourage women and
    girls to study and to have active careers in the
    mathematical sciences and to promote equal op-

portunity and the equal treatment of women and girls in the mathematical sciences.

Canadian Economics Association (CEA)
Department of Economics, Brock University
500 Glenridge Avenue
St. Catharines, ON L2S 3A1
Canada
(905) 688-5550, ext. 6225
Web site: http://economics.ca
The CEA is an organization of academic economists in Canada.

Canadian Mathematical Society (CMS)
209 - 1725 St. Laurent Boulevard
Ottawa, ON K1G 3V4
Canada
(613) 733-2662
Web site: http://cms.math.ca
The CMS promotes the advancement, discovery, learning, and application of mathematics in Canada.

International Mathematical Union (IMU)
Secretariat
Markgrafenstr. 32
D-10117 Berlin
Germany
http://www.mathunion.org
IMU is an international non-governmental and nonprofit scientific organization, with the purpose of promoting international cooperation in mathematics.

It also awards the Fields Medal, one of the most prestigious honors in the field.

Mathematical Association of America (MAA)
1529 18th Street NW
Washington, DC 20036-1358
(202) 387-5200
Web site: http://www.maa.org
The MAA is the largest professional society that focuses on mathematics accessible at the undergraduate level.

National Council of Teachers of Mathematics (NCTM)
1906 Association Drive
Reston, VA 20191-1502
(800) 235-7566
Web site: http://www.nctm.org
The NCTM is the public voice of mathematics education, supporting teachers to ensure equitable mathematics learning of the highest quality for all students.

National Educational Association (NEA)
1201 16th Street NW
Washington, DC 20036-3290
(202) 833-4000
http://www.nea.org
The NEA, the nation's largest professional employee organization, is committed to advancing the cause of public education at every level, from preschool to university graduate programs.

National Science Foundation (NSF)
4201 Wilson Boulevard
Arlington, VA 22230
(703) 292-5111
http://www.nsf.gov
The NSF is the primary federal agency supporting research at the frontiers of knowledge, across all fields of science and engineering and all levels of science and engineering education.

Society for Industrial and Applied Mathematics (SIAM)
3600 Market Street, 6th Floor
Philadelphia, PA 19104-2688
(215) 382-9800
Web site: http://siam.org
SIAM exists to ensure interactions between mathematics and other scientific and technological communities through membership activities, publication of journals and books, and conferences.

Web Sites

Due to the changing nature of Internet links, Rosen Publishing has developed an online list of Web sites related to the subject of this book. This site is updated regularly. Please use this link to access the list:

http://www.rosenlinks.com/STEM/Math

FOR FURTHER READING

American Library Association editors. *How to Get a Great Job*. New York, NY: Skyhorse Publishing, 2011.

Barrow, John D. *100 Essential Things You Didn't Know You Didn't Know: Math Explains Your World*. New York, NY: W.W. Norton & Co., 2010.

Bayer, Michael, et al. *Becoming an Urban Planner: A Guide to Careers in Planning and Urban Design*. Hoboken, NJ: Wiley, 2010.

Beshara, Tony. *Acing the Interview: How to Ask and Answer the Questions that Will Get You the Job*. New York, NY: AMACOM, 2008.

Bush, Pamela McCauley. *Transforming Your STEM Career Through Leadership and Innovation: Inspiration and Strategies for Women*. Waltham, MA: Academic Press, 2012.

Cole, George M. *Surveyor Reference Manual*. 5th ed. Belmont, CA: Professional Publications, Inc., 2009.

DK Publishing. *Help Your Kids with Math: A Visual Problem Solver for Kids and Parents*. New York, NY: DK Publishing, 2010.

Elwes, Richard. *Mathematics 1001: Absolutely Everything That Matters About Mathematics in 1001 Bite-Sized Explanations*. Buffalo, NY: Firefly Books, 2010.

Facts On File, Inc. *Discovering Careers: Math*. New York, NY: Ferguson's, 2011.

Farr, Michael. *The Quick Résumé and Cover Letter Book: Write and Use an Effective Résumé in Only One Day*. Indianapolis, IN: JIST Works, 2011.

Fitzgerald, Theresa. *Math Dictionary for Kids: The Essential Guide to Math Terms, Strategies, and Tables*. 3rd ed. Waco, TX: Prufrock Press, 2011.

Frenkel, Edward. *Love and Math: The Heart of Hidden Reality*. New York, NY: Basic Books, 2013.

Fung, Kaiser. *Numbers Rule Your World: The Hidden Influence of Probability and Statistics on Everything You Do*. New York, NY: McGraw-Hill, 2010.

Gowers, Timothy. *Mathematics: A Very Short Introduction*. New York, NY: Oxford University Press, 2002.

Gowers, Timothy, ed. *The Princeton Companion to Mathematics*. Princeton, NJ: Princeton University Press, 2008.

Hahn, Gerald J., and Necip Doganaksoy. *A Career in Statistics: Beyond the Numbers*. Hoboken, NJ: Wiley, 2011.

Jackson, Tom, ed. *Mathematics: An Illustrated History of Numbers*. New York, NY: Shelter Harbor Press, 2012.

Kolata, Gina, ed. *The New York Times Book of Mathematics: More Than 100 Years of Writing by the Numbers*. New York, NY: Sterling, 2013.

Lambert, Stephen. *Great Jobs for Business Majors.* New York, NY: McGraw-Hill, 2008.

Merzbach, Uta C., and Carl B. Boyer. *A History of Mathematics.* 3rd ed. Hoboken, NJ: Wiley, 2011.

Pickover, Clifford A. *The Math Book: From Pythagoras to the 57th Dimension, 250 Milestones in the History of Mathematics.* New York, NY: Sterling, 2012.

Reeves, Ellen Gordon. *Can I Wear My Nose Ring to the Interview? The Crash Course in Finding, Landing, and Keeping Your First Real Job.* New York, NY: Workman Publishing, 2009.

Ross, Stan, and James Carberry. *The Inside Track to Careers in Accounting.* New York, NY: AICPA, 2010.

Rumsey, Deborah J. *Statistics for Dummies.* 2nd ed. Hoboken, NJ: Wiley, 2011.

Silver, Nate. *The Signal and the Noise: Why So Many Predictions Fail—But Some Don't.* New York, NY: Penguin Press, 2012.

Stewart, Ian. *The Mathematics of Life.* New York, NY: Basic Books, 2013.

Stewart, Ian. *Visions of Infinity: The Great Mathematical Problems.* New York, NY: Basic Books, 2013.

Strogatz, Steven H. *The Joy of X: A Guided Tour of Math, From One to Infinity.* Boston, MA: Houghton Mifflin Harcourt, 2012.

Szabo, Fred. *Actuaries' Survival Guide: How to Succeed in One of the Most Desirable Professions.* 2nd ed. Waltham, MA: Academic Press, 2012.

Waldrep, Lee W. *Becoming an Architect: A Guide to Careers in Design.* 2nd ed. Hoboken, NJ: Wiley, 2010.

Yuki, Hiroshi. *Math Girls.* Austin, TX: Bento Books, Inc., 2011.

BIBLIOGRAPHY

American Astronomical Association. "Careers in Astronomy." September 2013. Retrieved September 2013 (http://aas.org/learn/careers -astronomy).

American Economics Association. "What Are the Fields in Economics?" Retrieved September 2013 (http://www.aeaweb.org/students/ Fields.php).

The American Institute of Certified Public Accountants. "Your Accounting Future Starts Here." 2013. Retrieved September 2013 (http:// www.startheregoplaces.com).

Bureau of Labor Statistics. *Occupational Outlook Handbook*. 2013. Retrieved September 2013 (http://www.bls.gov/ooh).

Capraro, Robert M., et al. (eds). *STEM Project-Based Learning: An Integrated Science, Technology, Engineering, and Mathematics (STEM) Approach*. Rotterdam, The Netherlands: Sense Publishers, 2013.

Cornell Astronomy Department. "Curious About Astronomy? Ask an Astronomer." December 18, 2011. Retrieved September 2013 (http:// curious.astro.cornell.edu/careers.php).

Council of Chief School Officers. "District of Columbia Mathematics Educator Named 2005 National Teacher of the Year at a White House Ceremony." April 19, 2005. Retrieved September 2013 (http://www.ccsso.org/ntoy/National_Teachers/ Teacher_Detail.html?id=351).

District of Columbia Public Schools. "Jason Kamras: Chief of Human Capital." 2012. Retrieved September 2013 (http://www.dc.gov/DCPS/About+DCPS/Who+We+Are/Leadership+Team/Jason+Kamras).

Drew, David E. *STEM the Tide: Reforming Science, Technology, Engineering, and Math Education in America.* Baltimore, MD: Johns Hopkins University Press, 2011.

Echaore-McDavid, Susan. *Career Opportunities in Science.* 2nd ed. New York, NY: Checkmark Books, 2008.

ETPRO. "Cryptologists/ Cryptanalyst." 2012. Retrieved September 2013 (www.edtechpolicy.org/cyberk12/Documents/CoolCareers/2012/lessons/crypto/careerhandoutCryptographer.pdf).

Ferguson Publishing Company. *Careers in Focus: Mathematics and Physics.* 2nd ed. New York, NY: Ferguson, 2008.

Forbes. "Quants: The Rocket Scientists of Wall Street." June 7, 2013. Retrieved September 2013 (http://www.forbes.com/sites/investopedia/2013/06/07/quants-the-rocket-scientists-of-wall-street).

Google.com. "Carrie Grimes." Retrieved September 2013 (http://research.google.com/pubs/author31907.html).

GovCentral. "Cryptanalyst." October 30, 2007. Retrieved September 2013 (http://govcentral

.monster.com/security-clearance-jobs/articles/
620-cryptanalyst).

Honey, Margaret, and David E. Kanter. *Design, Make, Play: Growing the Next Generation of STEM Innovators*. New York, NY: Routledge, 2013.

Lambert, Stephen E., and Ruth J. Decotis. *Great Jobs for Math Majors*. 2nd ed. New York, NY: McGraw-Hill, 2006.

Lohr, Steve. "For Today's Graduate, Just One Word: Statistics." *New York Times*, August 6, 2009. Retrieved September 2013 (http://www.nytimes.com/2009/08/06/technology/06stats.html).

Lorber, Laura. "So You Want to Be a Mortgage Loan Officer…" *FINS*, September 7, 2010. Retrieved September 2013 (http://www.fins.com/Finance/Articles/SB127619173585503937/So-You-Want-to-Be-a-Mortgage-Loan-Officer).

Lurie, Stephen. "How the Senate Exploits Unpaid Interns." *Atlantic*, August 29, 2013. Retrieved September 2013 (http://www.theatlantic.com/politics/archive/2013/08/shocked-shocked-the-senate-exploits-unpaid-interns/279111).

Manzoor, Sarfraz. "Quants: Meet the Math Geniuses Running Wall Street." *Business Insider*, July 23, 2013. Retrieved September 2013 (http://www.businessinsider.com/quants-meet-the-math-geniuses-running-wall-street-2013-7).

Moomaw, Sally. *Teaching STEM in the Early Years: Activities for Integrating Science, Technology,*

Engineering, and Mathematics. St. Paul, MN: Redleaf Press, 2013.

National Security Agency. "Career Fields: Crypt-analysis/Signals Analysis." January 15, 2009. Retrieved September 2013 (http://www.nsa.gov/careers/career_fields/cryptsiganalysis.shtml).

Oljace, Glory. *STEM Is Elementary: Why Elementary Science, Technology, Engineering, and Mathematics Prepares Students to Beat the Gaps!* Bethel, MN: STEM Is Elementary, LLC, 2012.

Silver, Nate. "FiveThirtyEight: Politics Done Right." FiveThirtyEight.com. Retrieved September 2013 (http://www.fivethirtyeight.com).

Smith, Jacquelyn. "The Highest-Paying STEM Jobs for Recent College Graduates." *Forbes*, June 27, 2013. Retrieved September 2013 (http://www.forbes.com/sites/jacquelynsmith/2013/06/27/the-highest-paying-stem-jobs-for-recent-college-graduates).

SOA/CAS. "Be an Actuary." 2013. Retrieved September 2013 (http://www.beanactuary.org).

Social Security Administration. "Actuarial Life Table." Retrieved September 2013 (http://www.ssa.gov/OACT/STATS/table4c6.html).

Statistics2013.org. "The International Year of Statistics." 2013. Retrieved September 2013 (http://www.statistics2013.org).

Stewart, Ian. *Letters to a Young Mathematician.* New York, NY: Basic Books, 2006.

Taylor, Marisa. "A Career in Accounting." *Wall Street Journal*, September 12, 2010. Retrieved September 2013 (http://online.wsj.com/article/SB 10001424052748704358904575547811120527 5920.html).

U.S. Department of Education. "Science, Technology, Engineering, and Math: Education for Global Leadership." Retrieved September 2013 (http://www.ed.gov/stem).

U.S. News and World Report. "Loan Officer Overview." 2013. Retrieved September 2013 (http://money.usnews.com/careers/best-jobs/loan -officer).

INDEX

About the Author

Corona Brezina is an author who has written over a dozen young adult books for Rosen Publishing. Several of her previous books have also focused on in-demand careers, including *Careers in Law Enforcement, Careers in Meteorology, Careers in Nanotechnology, Careers as a Medical Examiner, Careers in the Juvenile Justice System, Getting a Job in Health Care*, and *Jobs in Sustainable Energy*. She lives in Chicago.

Photo Credits

Designer: Brian Garvey; Editor: Shalini Saxena;
Photo Researcher: Karen Huang